Why not Embroider Letters?

Daphne J Ashby
& Jackie Woolsey

January 2002

DEDICATION

We are pleased to dedicate this work to our two delightful "supporters",
Ann Pearce and Jill Kempster,
to whom we are most grateful for their particular contributions to this book
and without whose help and support over many years
our lives would be less enriched.

Other books by the same authors:

Ribbon Embroidery
    published by David & Charles, Newton Abbott
    Hardback - September 1996, Paperback - August 1998

Creative Embroidery Techniques using Colour through Gold
    published by the Guild of Master Craftsman Publications Ltd.
    Lewes - June 1998

Why not make a Beaded Amulet Purse?
    self-published - June 1998

Why not Carry on Beading?
    self-published - June 1999

Stumpwork - Why Not?
    self-published - January 2001

Why not make a Box? (by Jackie)
    self-published - September 1996

Making Hand-Sewn Boxes (by Jackie)
    published by the Guild of Master Craftsman Publications Ltd.
    Lewes - April 1999

Copyright 2002 - Daphne J Ashby & Jackie Woolsey

This book first published in the UK in January 2002
by Daphne J Ashby & Jackie Woolsey
The Firs, Burgh St Peter, BECCLES NR34 0BU
email: jackiewoolsey@talk21.com

ISBN 0-9540030-1-2

Contents

Embroidered letters can be used effectively to create
very personal items and, in the photograph above,
the silk-embroidered P has been simply mounted,
the William Morris style design for the U
has been used to decorate a bag and
the G in gold work is shown on the lid of a box,
which is covered with co-ordinating fabrics.

INTRODUCTION

The letter shapes that we use today have evolved over many centuries, always influenced by the tools and materials available. The Sumerians, around 3500 BC, used wedge-shaped sticks to make their Cuneiform shapes, the Egyptians evolved their hieroglyphs using reed brushes and pens and the beautiful Greek and Roman alphabets were fashioned with chisels in stone and then square-cut reed pens/quills on vellum and parchment. It is the latter which form the basis of our Western writing.

Among the earliest manuscripts surviving for us to see is the Book of Kells in the Trinity College Library, Dublin, which Daphne and I recently visited. There we were able to admire the glorious illuminated letters occupying whole pages or as initials at the beginnings of words or paragraphs.

We know that letters have been used in embroidery in England for many centuries and we can see evidence of this on the 10th century stole and maniple of St Cuthbert in Durham Cathedral. Ecclesiastical vestments offer fine examples of embroidered lettering all over the world and the famous Bayeux Tapestry from the 12th century demonstrates all too clearly the visual value of words and pictures. Stitch samplers have also often incorporated lettering, particularly names and dates as well as verses.

In this book, using needles and fabrics, letters have been given individual treatment and Daphne and Ann have each embroidered a complete alphabet. Ann has shown how a uniform set of letters can be simply stitched to give each one its own special character. Daphne has managed to find enough different techniques or styles to enable her to design and embroider an entire alphabet of highly individual letters to stunning effect.

The intention of our book is not that the reader should slavishly copy the techniques but adapt ideas or parts of the designs to use on different letters or styles of letters. For this purpose we have also provided several alphabets which can be enlarged on the photocopier to provide the starting point for individual designs.

In our daily lives, we are surrounded by letters, mostly in the form of words, which are informative, instructive or descriptive but only rarely purely decorative. We hope that, through the pages of this book, you will find the inspiration to bring the beauty of individual embroidered letters into your personal surroundings.

Jackie Woolsey

1

ANNIE'S ALPHABET

We are grateful to our mutual friend and embroiderer, Ann Pearce from Audlem, Vice-President of the South Cheshire Branch of the Embroiderers' Guild, for contributing the complete alphabet of embroidered letters which follows and for the helpful notes which accompany each one.

Much use was made of a variety of books for design inspiration, enabling the ideas to be simple but attractive.

Use an air/water (Madeira Magic Pen) to mark the letters and designs onto the chosen fabrics - the drawn lines will vanish within 24 hours or can be removed using a fine brush dipped in water.   Do not use felt-tipped pens for the purpose.

Bondaweb was ironed onto the back of the polycotton gold fabric chosen for the actual letters. The letters forming the master alphabet used in this section were traced and the tracings positioned in reverse onto the Bondaweb and outlined before cutting out.   See pages 16 and 17, which follow this section, for templates of the alphabet used, which can be enlarged on a photocopier to the size required.

Remove the paper from the Bondaweb and iron the letter onto the chosen background fabric - a cotton damask was used throughout this section.

When using Bondaweb, make sure that the gum side of the Bondaweb is against the fabric.   Before ironing, cover the whole design with silicon paper to prevent the iron getting sticky.

Back the fabric with a piece of muslin or thin cotton and put this double layer into a small, round embroidery frame, making sure to maintain the straight grain of the fabric. The fabric will be held more firmly if the inner ring of the frame is bound with cotton tape.

In most instances the design was applied over the letters by tracing using tissue paper and then stitching through the tissue paper and tearing the paper away, leaving the outline.   (Use pincers for accuracy in removing the paper.)   If appropriate, the decorative design can be drawn directly onto the letter and fabric, again using the "vanishing" pen.

The embroidery for all the letters in this section uses stranded cotton and only a single strand unless otherwise indicated.

Letter A

Stem: work in stem stitch in green Anchor 462 using two strands.

Flower petals: lazy-daisy or open chain stitch in 4 strands blue DMC 813 & darker blue Anchor 484.

Flower centres: French knots in yellow Anchor 443 in six strands.

Letter B

The design outline was traced onto tissue paper and stitched through onto the fabric using stranded cotton in the chosen colours.
Main petals: satin-stitch in pinks Anchor 746, 403, 402.
Inner petals: cream Anchor 885.
French knot stamens: yellow Anchor 443 using 3 strands.
Leaves: satin-stitch & stem stitch in green Anchor 462.

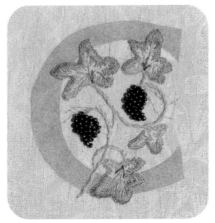

Letter C

This grapevine was traced and out-lined onto the fabric by backstitch-ing around design, tearing the tissue paper away and buttonholing over the back stitch using a single strand of green Anchor 497.

Stem: work in stem stitch in green Anchor 462 using two strands.

The grapes are tiny beads.

Letter D

Stems: work two rows of stem stitch in green Anchor 462.

Bud: satin-stitch, lazy daisy and fly stitch using green Anchor 462.

Flowers: French knots using six strands of blue Anchor 506 & 760.

Leaves: satin-stitch in green Anchor 462, 497 and 498.

Letter E

This simple design was drawn straight onto the fabric using a "vanishing" pen.

Stems: worked in stem stitch in two strands of brown with complementary beads from an old necklace.

Letter F

Flower petals: work in lazy-daisy stitch using 3 strands of Anchor multicolour 1325.

Leaves & stem: stem stitch in 2 strands green Anchor 497.

Multi-coloured beads to decorate.

Letter G

Roses: worked in satin-stitch using pink Anchor 402 and 403.

Stems: stem stitch in green Anchor 497 and brown Anchor 280, using two strands.

Leaves: satin-stitch in green Anchor 497.

Letter H

Holly leaves: outline first in back stitch and then fill with satin-stitch in green Anchor 497 and 498 .

Red glass beads are positioned to represent the berries.

Letter I

Gold star-shaped sequins, topped with gold seed beads, are sewn in a spiral shape to create this design.

Letter J

The fly-agaric mushroom caps are Vilene, which has been car-sprayed red. These were then stem stitched in place with a single strand of red Anchor 041 and grey DMC 648. Decorate the caps with small white beads.

The mushroom stalks are acrylic-painted Vilene held in place with grey DMC 648 and Anchor 589 & 590 using stem stitch and two strands.

Fungus base: satin-stitch in fawn.

Letter K

Loganberries: French knots using 3 strands of red multi-coloured Anchor 107.

Leaves: cut out from green fabric and herringbone-stitched in place - two strands of green Anchor 467.

Outline leaves with backstitch in green Anchor 467 .

Stems: stem stitch using 467.

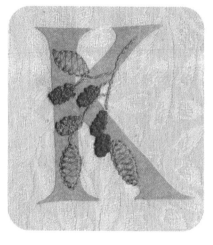

Letter L

Ivy leaves: dyed green fabric Bondawebbed onto white cotton and then the shapes cut out.

The leaves are stitched down and the veins created in backstitch using green Anchor 498 1 strand.

Stems: stem stitch again in green Anchor 498 using two strands.

Letter M

Leaves: satin-stitch in green Anchor 496 & 497.

Stems: stem stitch, also in Anchor 496 & 497, using two strands.

Use seed beads and larger beads to decorate.

Letter N

Peach and the leaves:car-sprayed iron-on Vilene was used and then Bondawebbed, cut out and ironed in position.

Stitching: all stem stitch using a single strand.
Peach: orange Anchor 537
                     and 538
Leaves: green Anchor 467
Branch: brown Anchor 478

Letter O

The design used for this letter is based on a Venetian lace pattern.

Stitches: stem stitch, satin-stitch, chain stitch, fly stitch, French knots (six strands) and seeding.

Threads: green Anchor 497 and 498 and multi-coloured DMC 1335.

Letter P

Dyed silk was Bondawebbed onto cotton fabric and then the butterfly, flower and leaves were cut out.

The underneath leaves and petals were placed in position and held down with small stitches.

The front petals and the butterfly wings are held down with tiny French knots.

The leaves are held in place with stem stitch and French knots.   The stem is worked in stem stitch using green Anchor 498.

The body, head and antennae of the butterfly are worked using single strand black back stitch and bronze and black beads.

Letter Q

Flower head: French knots in mauve Anchor 584 and 585.

Leaves: stem stitch in green Anchor 280, 732 & cream.

Bulb: stem stitch in two strands brown Anchor 0369 and cream.

Roots: stem stitch in two strands grey Anchor 590.

Letter R - Roger's red rose:

Roses: dark red ribbon petals made using 1¼" lengths of 3mm silk ribbon and a single strand. See Stitch Glossary for details on how to work this stitch.

Stalks: backstitch in green Anchor 497.

Leaves: satin-stitch in green Anchor 498 & 700.

Small gold petit beads are stitched at the centres of the roses.

Letter S

Car-sprayed stiff Vilene is used for the sun-flower and its leaves. Red and yellow for the sunflower's petals, green for the leaves, and the shapes cut out.
Detail on the leaves was created using acrylic paint and backstitch - green Anchor 497.
Stem: stem stitch in green Anchor 497.
The petals are secured with a single stitch at the inside point, starting with the outside circle and working inwards.
Once the flower has been built up, the centre is formed with beads - three colours were used here.

Letter T

This is the letter T featured on the cover.

The curves are achieved by positioning a 1p coin on alternate sides.

The resulting curves are stem stitched using two strands of rust brown DMC 919.

Beads in a similar colour are stitched in position on alternate sides of the curves.

Letter T

The letter T lends itself naturally to the tree shape and this T is offered as an alternative. Dyed green silk fabric is bonded onto iron-on Vilene and the leaf shapes cut out to utilise varying colours.
The trunk and branches are worked in stem stitch: 2 strands of brown Anchor 478 and green Anchor 732.
The leaf shapes are attached using small beads.

Letter U

This design has been based on a detail from an Elizabethan embroidery.

The lozenge shapes are filled with couched threads in a lattice pattern. The satin-stitch is in red Anchor 476. The French knots use three strands of Anchor 732.

Other threads used were brown Anchor 478 and green Anchor 280.

Letter V

The leaves are outlined in stem stitch and fly stitch using four strands of green Anchor 498 with French knots added.

Pale and dark green beads are carefully positioned around the outside.

Letter W

This design is based on part of an ancient embroidery.

The laid threads (six strands) have been couched with a single strand of mauve Anchor 0101 & 587.

Gold ribbon was stitched in position and gold sequins applied with gold beads.

Letter X

Leaves: worked in satin-stitch.
Leaf veins: back stitch.

Flower stems: stem stitch.
Flower petals are blue beads and the
stamens bronze beads.

All the stitches have been worked using
multi-coloured DMC 92.

Letter Y

Flowers: worked in buttonhole stitch in
two strands of pinks Anchor 746 & 438.

Stamen heads: French knots in three
strands of yellow Anchor 487 with bronze
seed beads for the centres.

Stems: stem stitch in green Anchor 498.

Leaves: chain stitch in two strands of
green Anchor 496 & 498.

Letter Z

Cream snowflake-design glittered
fabric was painted pale blue with
weak acrylic paint.

Iron-on Vilene was applied to the
back of the fabric and the
snowflake shapes cut out and the
veins drawn in gold pen.

The snowflakes are held in place
with gold seed beads and further
beads added to enhance the
decoration.

This is the alphabet of letters used as templates for the embroideries in Annie's Section - pages 3 - 11

These letters may be photocopied and enlarged to the size required.

Alternative alphabets in Cross Stitch and Back Stitch

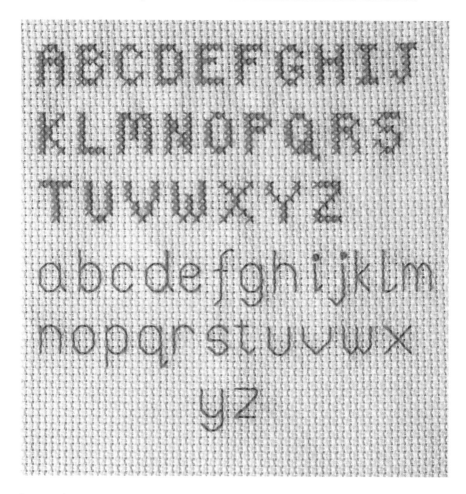

Letters in cross stitch

A study of old samplers will reveal that the names of the stitchers and the dates on which they worked their samplers were more often than not executed in cross stitch and this remains a very popular stitch today, although its use is far more creative in the present day.

For the purpose of lettering of this type, it is important that the cross stitches are worked on an evenweave fabric and, in the examples shown, an Aida fabric was used.

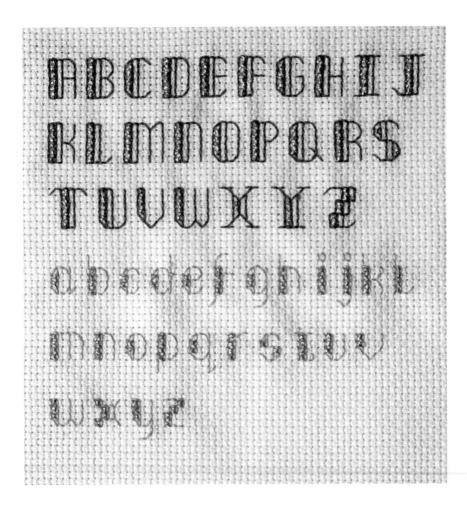

In the first alphabet, the upper case characters are in cross stitch and the lower case in simple back stitches but, in the second, the letters are outlined in back stitch with cross stitches as filling. A single strand of stranded cotton has been used throughout with a gold metallic thread for the cross stitch in the second alphabet.

The order of stitching cross stitches is a personal choice but it is most important to ensure that the top stitch of the cross always lies in the same direction throughout a piece of work. Try to avoid taking the thread across an unembroidered area at the back of a piece of work so that there is no possibility that these threads might show through the fabric at the front.

ALTERNATIVE ALPHABETS

You will not necessarily use the specific letters we have chosen for the various projects. However, we offer below a selection of alphabets which can be enlarged to the size you require and then traced. There are, of course, many alphabets and styles of lettering available from books and on the computer.

A B C D E F G H I J
K L M N O P Q R S
T U V W X Y Z

𝕬 𝕭 𝕮 𝕯 𝕰 𝕱
𝕲 𝕳 𝕴 𝕵 𝕶 𝕷
𝕸 𝕹 𝕺 𝕻 𝕼 𝕽
𝕾 𝕿 𝖀 𝖁 𝖂 𝖃
𝖄 𝖅

A B C D E F G
H I J K L M N O
P Q R S T U V
X Y Z

A B C D E F G H I J K L M N
O P Q R S T U V W X Y Z

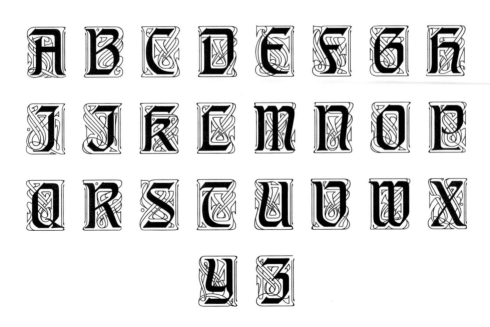

DAPHNE'S EMBROIDERED LETTERS

The letters in the following section use different styles of lettering. Many embroidery techniques have been employed and these include:

Traditional techniques

B	Gold work	E	Assisi
L	Stumpwork	N	Pulled thread
P	Long & short shading	V	Casalguidi
W	Blackwork	X	Cross stitch
Y	Hardanger		

Those involving surface stitchery

C	Variety of stitches	G	Couching
K	Pattern darning	Q	Ribbon
S	Chain stitch		

Applique

O   French knots, shading and applied fabric
Z   Applied fabric, ribbon and quilting

Beading

I   Brick stitch beadwork and appliqued leaves
M   Loom beading

Canvas work stitches on Congress Cloth

A   Bargello
D   Triple rice and tent stitch
T   Colour through Gold

Machine Embroidery

H   Shading, outlining and applied beads

Computer designed

J   Shaded and zig-zag back stitch

Design Styles

F   Chinese
R   Elizabethan
U   William Morris

Although each letter has been worked in a specific style, it would not be difficult to adapt the stitches and background to a different letter.

Letter A

The gold kid letter A is stitched onto the Bargello background.

Remembering that, in canvas work, vertical and horizontal stitches do not cover the fabric as well as diagonal stitches, the needle contained four rayon threads which are doubled to give eight thicknesses.

Materials

       8" square Congress Cloth
       Gutermann Dekor 100% Viscosa threads:

Dark Green	8840
Medium Green	8320
Pale Blue	6260
Lemon	1460
Tan	1956

Gutermann 100% Polyester Dekor Metallic effect thread - Gold No. 24
Gold kid for letter A
Extra heavy interfacing for lining
Two-colour couching thread in gold and white

Equipment

   8" square wooden embroidery frame
   Sharp embroidery scissors
   No. 24 tapestry needle

Preparation

Stretch the Congress Cloth over the wooden embroidery frame, securing it
with either staples or drawing pins.   If drawing pins are used, cover the
heads with masking tape to avoid the rayon threads catching on them.   On
the top edge of the Congress cloth, mark the centre of the fabric.

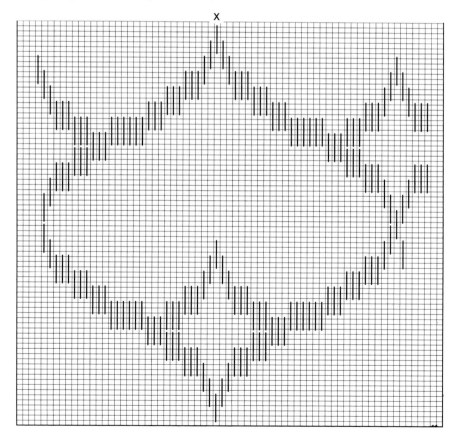

Embroidery

Measure and mark a point 1½" to the left of the centre of the Congress cloth and 1" down.   Starting at point X on the chart and at the mark just made, work the outline of the shapes in the gold metallic thread (a single thread doubled in the needle), carefully following the chart, until the gold outlines shown have been completed.   Each vertical straight stitch is over six threads on the Congress Cloth.

Then, working inside the gold outline, stitch the following rows:

Row 1   Four threads of dark green
Row 2   Two of dark green plus two of medium green
Row 3   Four threads of medium green
Row 4   Two of medium green plus two of pale blue
Row 5   Four threads of pale blue
Row 6   Two threads pale blue and two of lemon
Row 7   Gold metallic thread - this time the stitches divide in the middle and go upwards and downwards.   The resulting space is filled with tan stitches.

Carry on stitching in this way until the desired space has been filled.   The illustrated background to the letter 'A' measures approximately 5½" wide x 6" high.

Cut out the desired letter in gold kid (remember to reverse the outline when marking it on the back of the kid) and a slightly smaller version in extra heavy inter-facing.

Position the interfacing and stitch in place.   Then lay the gold kid exactly over the top of the letter.

The letter in the photograph is couched in place around all sides using two-colour couching thread and a Viscosa thread.

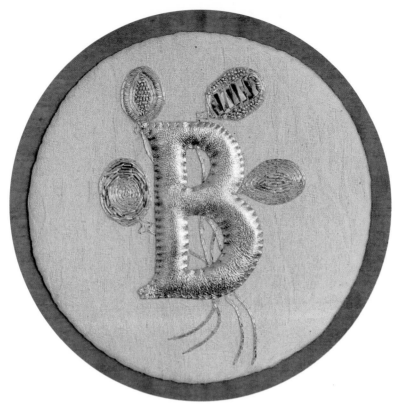

Letter B

Traditional gold work is used for the letter B.   The letter itself is cut out in gold kid, which is laid over a layer of felt and stitched to the background fabric.   Traditional gold threads are added as decoration.

Materials
10" square of background fabric - cotton damask is used here
Rectangle of gold kid, large enough for the letter B
Rectangle of yellow felt, similar size
Gold threads: small amounts of the following:
       Imitation Jap gold
       Bright check Gilt No. 3
       Bright check Gilt No. 6
       Smooth gilt purl No. 6
       Gold plate
Gold metalic petite seed beads
Madeira gold metallic thread No. 30 for couching

Reel of gold sewing thread
Circle of Vilene extra heavy interfacing
Gutermann sewing thread gold 968

Equipment

8" circular wooden embroidery frame   Fine embroidery needle
Sharp embroidery scissors   Tracing paper
Scissors for cutting metallic threads   Sharp pencil

Preparation

Trace the letter B and cut it out in the gold kid.   Cut the letter in felt but
make it slightly smaller all round.

Trace the design around the letter and, following the design, tack the tracing
onto the background fabric.   Run the needle along the line of stitching and
remove the tracing paper.

Embroidery

Tack the felt in position and lay the kid over the felt. With Gutermann gold sewing thread, stitch the gold kid down, coming up through the background fabric alongside the letter and going down through the kid.

Outline each of the balloons and strings with the Jap gold, laying a double strand and couching over them with the Madeira gold thread. Take the ends down through the background fabric, cut and stitch them down neatly.

Going from left to right, start to decorate balloon No. 1. This has a spiral of Jap gold (again used double) in the centre and is surrounded by smooth gilt purl, cut in short lengths and threaded on like bugle beads.

Balloon No. 2 has a single length of Bright check Gilt No. 3, which is again threaded on like a long bead - catch this in place to keep a good curve. Follow this with two double lines of Jap gold and fill the remaining space with the petite gold beads in rows.

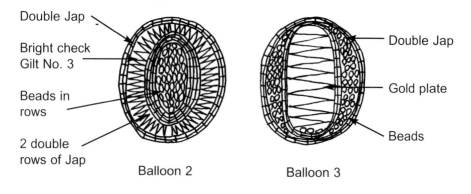

Double Jap

Bright check
Gilt No. 3

Beads in
rows

2 double
rows of Jap

Balloon 2

Double Jap

Gold plate

Beads

Balloon 3

The next balloon, No. 3, is decorated with gold plate, which is laid down the centre. Bend a small end under and attach the plate with a stitch. Fold it over and stitch about 1 cm. away. Fold back and stitch. Keep doing this until you reach the bottom of the balloon. Surround this area with a double Jap gold couched in place and fill the area between this row and the outside edge with the petite beads.

Balloon No. 4 is couched with four double rows of Jap gold around the out-side. The remaining space is filled with cut lengths of Bright check Gilt No. 6, stitched on as beads. The background fabric is then stretched and laced over a circle of interfacing and the finished piece stitched onto a contrasting background.

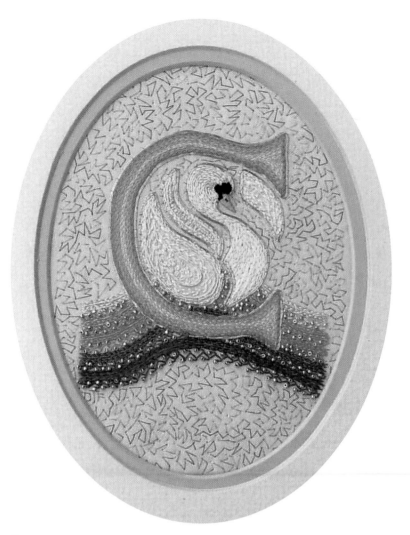

Letter C

The letter C is worked in rows of chain stitch with the deep orange on the outside edge and the mid-orange, yellow and cream shading inwards.

The head and body of the swan are worked in rows of stem stitch and the beak in satin-stitch.

The outlines of the letter C and the head, body and the wing shapes of the swan are all couched using the gold edging.

Materials

10" square of cotton background fabric
Indian rayon threads:

White	Deep orange
Cream	Mid orange
Yellow	4 shades of turquoise
Black	

Madeira metallic thread No. 6 - gold 43 (couched edging)
Madeira metallic embroidery thread - Astro 2
1 black bead for the eye
1 packet Bead Design gold petite beads 4068
Oval aperture card
Extra heavy interfacing - slightly larger than the size of the
aperture of the mount

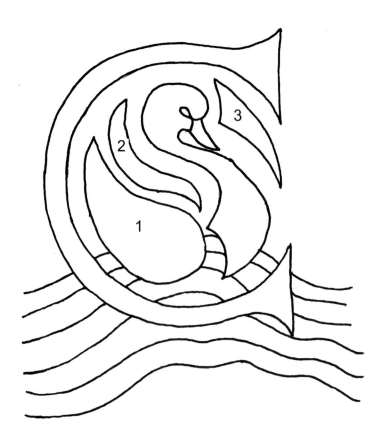

Equipment

8" Circular wooden embroidery frame   Sharp embroidery scissors
Fine embroidery needle   Tracing paper
Beading needle   Sharp pencil

Preparation

Stretch the background fabric tightly into the embroidery frame. Trace the letter C and the design and transfer this onto the fabric by tacking along the lines and then removing the tracing paper.

Embroidery

Outline the letter C in deep orange chain stitch, gradually shading more rows of chain stitch inwards using the mid-orange, yellow and cream.

Work the head and body of the swan in rows of stem stitch and the beak in satin-stitch with tiny French knots for the area between the beak and the eye, which is a black bead. Lay Madeira No. 6 - gold 43 around the outlines of the letter C and the head, body of the swan and couch into place.

The largest shape 1 is edged in chain stitch, followed by two rows of stem stitch, a row of feather stitching and a further row of chain stitch. The remaining space is filled with French knots. Shape 2 is edged with chain stitch and a row of stem stitch and then the centre is filled with a row of Vandyke stitch. The remaining shape 3 is edged in chain stitch, followed by a row of feather stitch and a row of stem stitch, the space left filled with French knots. Outline these three areas in gold thread.

The waves are worked in cream and the four shades of turquoise, starting with the deepest shade of turquoise at the bottom. Each wave is worked in:

     1 row of chain stitch
     1 row of stem stitch
     1 row of chain stitch
     1 row of stem stitch
     1 row of feather stitch

A bead is then added to each point on the feather stitch.
A piece of extra heavy interfacing is attached to the back of the work and zig-zag back stitching is worked all round the edges of the design in metallic embroidery thread.

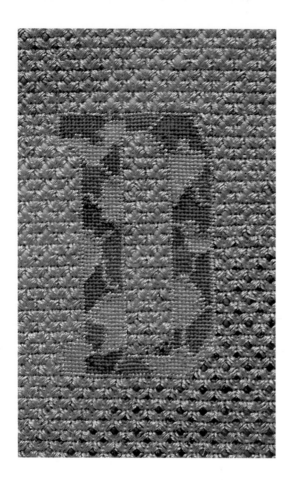

Letter D

This "Colour through Gold" design is worked on Congress Cloth using Madeira Rayon Thread No. 40 and Madeira Gold Metallic thread No. 12 . Only two canvas work stitches are used throughout.

Materials

8½" x 6" piece of Congress Cloth

Madeira Rayon Thread No. 40 - 1 reel each of:

Cerise	1110
Dark turquoise	1280
Pale turquoise	1045
Deep yellow	1065
Mid yellow	1024

2 reels Madeira Gold metallic thread No. 12, colour 33

Equipment

8½" x 6" rectangular wooden embroidery frame
No. 24 tapestry needle   Sharp embroidery scissors

Preparation

Stretch the Congress Cloth over the wooden embroidery frame securing it with either staples or drawing pins. If drawing pins are used, cover the heads with masking tape to avoid the threads catching on them.

Embroidery

Mark out the letter D onto the canvas. To make it easy to work, use a count that can be divided by 6. The diagram illustrating the letter D shows how this is done.

1	1	1	2	2	2	3	3	3	4	4	4
1	1	2	2	2	3	3	3	4	4	4	5
1	2	2	2	3	3	3	4	4	4	5	5
2	2	2	3	3	3	4	4	4	5	5	5
2	2							5	5	5	6
2	3	3			4	4			5	6	6
3	3	3			4	5			6	6	6
3	3	4			5	5			6	6	7
3	4	4			5	5			6	7	7
4	4	4			5	6			7	7	7
4	4	5			6	6			7	7	8
4	5	5			6	6			7	8	8
5	5	5			6	7			8	8	8
5	5	6			7	7			8	8	9
5	6	6			7	7			8	9	9
6	6							8	9	9	9
6	6	7	7	7	8	8	8	9	9	9	10
6	7	7	7	8	8	8	9	9	9	10	10
7	7	7	8	8	8	9	9	9	10	10	10
7	7	8	8	8	9	9	9	10	10	10	10

☐ Each single square represents 3 threads

| 1 | Each square containing a number (1 - 10) represents one Triple Rice Stitch over 6 threads |

The background is worked in triple rice stitch and each stitch is over 6 threads.

Outline the whole letter in tent stitch using one gold metallic thread doubled. Divide the inside of the letter into small areas, which are again outlined in gold tent stitch.

These areas are then filled with tent stitch in three of the colours in use - in this case, the two turquoise and the cerise thread are used. (Work with three rayon threads in the needle doubled to give six thicknesses.)

Decide on the size of the background area to surround the letter - again the count needs to be divisible by 6.

Work the large main crosses of the triple rice stitch (see the Stitch Glossary - page 111) using the coloured threads (three doubled to give 6 thicknesses) in sets of three diagonally, as shown on the chart on the previous page, in the folowing colour combinations:

1	3 cerise
2	2 cerise + 1 mid yellow
3	3 mid yellow
4	2 mid yellow + 1 deep yellow
5	2 deep yellow + 1 pale turquoise
6	3 pale turquoise
7	2 pale turquoise + 1 dark turquoise
8	3 dark turquoise
9	2 dark turquoise+ 1 cerise
10	3 cerise

The gold metallic thread stitches are then worked over each corner of the coloured crosses as shown on page 111 in the Stitch Glossary.

For more information regarding the "Colour through Gold" technique, see:

"Creative Embroidery Techniques using Colour Through Gold"
by Daphne J Ashby & Jackie Woolsey
pub. by the Guild of Master Craftsman Publications Ltd.
Lewes, East Sussex   1998

ISBN 1-86108-087-5

Letter E

This letter is worked using the technique known as Assisi work. This traditionally has the subject voided - in this case the capital letter - and a background of cross stitch, which would have been worked in red, blue or green and a fancy border. The example is worked on Hardanger fabric using flower thread - if you have difficulty in getting this thread, any single thread can be substituted.

Materials
       10" x 8" piece of Hardanger fabric
       1 skein each of black and cerise flower thread
       1 reel Madeira Gold metallic thread No. 12, colour 33

Equipment
       10" x 8" rectangular wooden embroidery frame
       Sharp embroidery scissors
       No. 24 tapestry needle

Preparation
Stretch the Hardanger fabric tightly onto the frame and attach using either staples or drawing pins. If drawing pins are used, cover these with masking tape to avoid the threads catching on them.

31

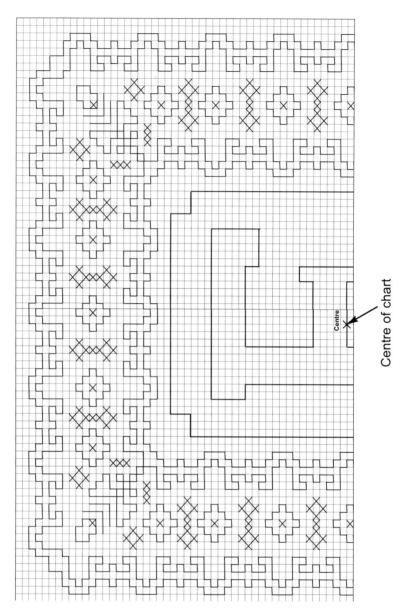

Centre of chart

Embroidery

Mark the centre of the fabric and start to back stitch the outline of the letter using a single strand of black thread. Using a piece of white cotton thread, outline the area to be filled with cross stitch (this will be removed later) and work the crosses. Remember always to start each stitch by working in the same direction.

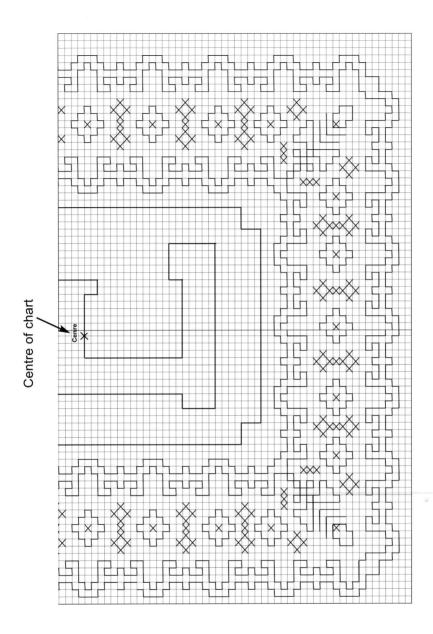

Centre of chart

Centre

The black outlines of the border are worked in back stitch, noting that the inside border corners are not the same as the outside border corners. Work the cerise diamonds of stitching next, noting again that some of these are differently spaced to fit in the border.   The gold crosses can then be added.

Letter F

A Chinese style has been adopted for this letter, which is mostly worked in satin-stitch. The fish, so often featured in this type of embroidery, is worked in silk and is surrounded with wave shapes.

Materials

10" square of crystal chiffon
10" square of cotton backing fabric
Pearsall's Filoselle Embroidery Silk - one skein each of:

White	088	Orange Yellow	154
Moonlight	316	Scarlet	021
China Blue	209	Scarlet	022

Equipment

8" circular wooden embroidery frame	Sharp pencil
Fine embroidery needle	Tracing paper
Sharp embroidery scissors	

Preparation

Trace the design and place the tracing under the centre of the cotton fabric and mark with a sharp pencil. Place the crystal chiffon on the top - the pencil lines will show through. Stretch onto the circular embroidery frame.

Embroidery

Outline the letter and wave shapes in one strand of the silk in the China Blue 209 using back stitch. This will give a good edge to the embroidery which is worked over it.

Use the photograph of the finished example for the placing of the colours.

All the embroidery is worked in a single strand of silk.

The wave shapes are worked entirely in satin-stitch using white 088, moonlight 316 and china blue 209.

The fish scales are outlined in blanket stitch using Orange Yellow 154. The space that remains is filled with Scarlet 021 and then three or four straight stitches are worked on the top in Scarlet 022.

The two fins are worked in the same three colours, using long and short stitch and starting at the outside with 154.

The tail is worked in 154 and satin-stitch.

The head is stitched in rows of stem stitch and the eye is a China Blue 209 French knot surrounded by straight stitches in White 088.

The letter has rounds or part-round shapes, each surrounded by blanket stitch in Scarlett 022 and the centres are French knots worked in Scarlet 022, China Blue 209 and Orange Yellow 154.

The background is worked in bars of satin-stitch in Scarlet 021 and China Blue 209. The China Blue 209 thread is also used to outline the letter in stem stitch.

Letter G

This letter is cut from gold kid which is stitched over a padding of felt. The decoration, in the shape of three rectangles, is all couching over mostly Kreinik and Coats threads, with the addition of a Madeira gold Jap-type thread and gold beads. There are many different types of gold braid, thread, ribbon, etc., which can be substituted for those mentioned in the materials list.

Materials

10" square of cotton background fabric
Piece of gold kid large enough to cut out the letter G
Yellow felt of the same size
A selection of gold threads and braids, including:

Kreinik Balger 1/8" ribbon 002
Coats Diadem
Kreinik Fine braid 202 HL
Madeira Gold No. 6, gold 43
Madeira Gold No. 30, gold 6033
Metallic gold seed beads
Glass gold Delica beads
Gutermann sewing thread gold 968

Equipment

8" circular wooden embroidery frame   Sharp pencil
Fine embroidery needle   Tracing paper
Beading needle   Sharp embroidery scissors
Large darning needle (to use for making a hole for the braids and thicker threads)

Preparation

Trace the design and place the tracing on top of the cotton fabric which is stretched on the wooden frame.   Tack the design through the paper and fabric and then tear away the tracing paper.

Embroidery

Cut out the letter shape in gold kid and a second one in the felt, which is slightly smaller.

Stitch the felt shape onto the cotton fabric and then place the gold kid shape over it and stitch evenly round the edge, coming up through the background fabric and going down into the gold kid using the Gutermann sewing thread.

The couching throughout is worked using the Madeira Gold No. 30.

The gold Kreinik Balger ribbon is couched around the outside of the rectangular shapes, followed by the Madeira Gold No. 6 which is used as a double thread and couched.

A length of gold Kreinik Fine braid is doubled and twisted to make a cord, which is then couched in place.

Then a second double row of Madeira Gold No. 6 is couched before the Coats Diadem is stitched on by adding the metallic gold beads at even intervals.

Another double Madeira Gold No. 6 is finally couched on.

The inside and outside edges of each of the rectangles then has a border of beads applied, which are couched in groups of three.

Using the beading needle and Madeira Gold No. 30, thread on a few glass gold Delica beads and, using the embroidery needle with Madeira Gold No. 30, couch over the beading thread between groups of three beads.

Letter H

Machine embroidery is used for this letter. French knots are combined with beads for the raised centre of the Hellenium flower.

The outline of the letter is couched with a thicker thread.

Materials

10" square of cotton background fabric
Piece of extra heavy interfacing - slightly larger than the aperture of the
          mount to be used
Machine embroidery thread -   3 shades of green   Mauve
                                 4 shades of yellow
Fine Madeira Gold metallic thread
Couching thread to outline the letter
Small amount of tan seed beads   Oval aperture card
Tan embroidery thread for French knots

Equipment

8" circular wooden embroidery frame   Sharp pencil
Embroidery needle   Sewing machine
Beading needle   Tracing paper
Sharp embroidery scissors

Preparation

Stretch the background fabric tightly into the frame, keeping the fabric at the bottom of the frame - place the larger ring on the table, add the fabric and stretch with the smaller ring.   Drop the lower feed teeth on the machine and remove the presser foot.

Trace the design and place this on top of the fabric. Machine round the design using yellow thread for the letter and flower, green for the leaves and stem. Remove the tracing paper.

Embroidery

Thread the machine with the palest yellow and the fine gold thread. With care you can machine with two threads through the needle.

Start machining at the top of the letter and work about a quarter of the way down before changing the yellow to the next shade.

Keep changing the yellow until all four shades have been used and you have reached the lower edge of the letter.

Next machine-stitch the mauve background to the letter.

The flower should be worked next - outline the petals and then shade them. The example used a matt thread for the outline and edging to the petals and a shiny thread for the middle. Do not stitch the flower centre.

Outline the leaves with the palest green and also stitch the centre vein.

Start the shading from the outside using the same thread. Working from the palest to the darkest shade, complete the shading.

Finally, rethread with the palest green and go over the central vein and add some side veins.

Place the extra heavy interfacing centrally behind the fabric and machine with the fine gold thread in a zig-zag line all over the background.

The tan seed beads can now be added at the base of the flower centre and then the French knots on the top, using the tan embroidery thread.

The thicker couching thread can now be used to edge the letter round the mauve background area, using the fine Madeira gold metallic thread for couching.

Letter I

This letter is made entirely with beads and then decorated with bought velvet ivy leaves.

The stems are worked using DMC No. 8 perle thread, which is couched with a single strand of Madeira stranded silk.

Materials

Seed beads - 1 packet each of green, yellow, brown, white and gold
Nymo D black beading thread
1 ball DMC No. 8 perle thread 3348
1 skein Madeira silk 1408
Velvet ivy leaves in two sizes (see List of Suppliers on page 112)
10" square silk background fabric
Extra heavy interfacing 6½" x 4½"

Equipment

8" circular wooden embroidery frame   Beading needle
Embroidery needle   Sharp embroidery scissors

Preparation

Stretch the silk tightly on the frame.

Beading

To work the top of the letter, select gold and brown seed beads.   Cut a
fairly generous length of the beading thread and, using a beading needle,
thread on 1 gold, 1 brown and 1 gold seed bead and pull the needle
through, leaving about six inches of thread hanging.   Hold these beads
firmly vertically between the thumb and finger of the left hand.

Pick up another set of three beads on the needle, pull the thread through the
beads and fold the thread so that the two sets lie side by side between the
fingers.   Take the needle up through the first set again and down through
the second set.

Keep working in this way, threading on three more beads, going through the
previous set of beads and through the one that has just been added.   Do
this until you have 14 sets of three beads lying side by side.

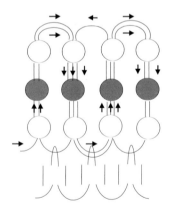

Then add another row of seed beads each side, by picking up a single gold
bead, taking the needle up behind and over the thread between the next two
beads of the previous row and going back down through the seed bead.

When you have worked a row along the top, work a row below the sets of
three.   By going into the threads between the beads, you will only have 13
beads in this row.   You are now ready to start the pattern using the chart.

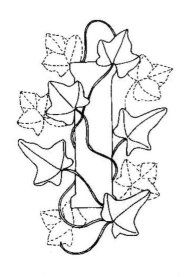

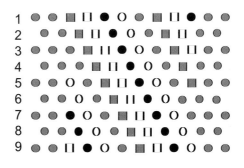

1	○	○	■	I I	●	O	○	■	I I	●	○	○
2		○	○	■	I I	●	O	○	■	I I	●	○	○
3	○	○	○	■	I I	●	O	○	■	I I	○	○
4		○	○	○	■	I I	●	O	○	■	○	○
5	○	○	O	○	■	I I	●	O	○	■	○	○
6		○	○	O	○	■	I I	●	O	○	○	○
7	○	○	●	O	○	■	I I	●	O	○	○	○
8		○	○	●	O	○	■	I I	●	O	○	○
9	○	○	I I	●	O	○	■	I I	●	O	○	○

- ○ Gold
- ■ Green
- I I Yellow
- ● Brown
- O White

Work row 1 and then turn the work round and work row 2. When you start row 3 and every alternate row, you will add two beads and then work as before but only going back through one of them.

At the end of row 3 and every alternate row, you will go into the thread which lies after the last bead of the previous row.

Keep working like this until you have worked 53 rows.

You will then add six beads (gold, brown, gold, gold, brown, gold) and then go up through the thread between the beads of the previous row and back down through just the last three beads. Work until you reach the end of the row, when you will have 14 sets of 3 beads. Work a row at the bottom just using gold beads.

The letter is now ready to stitch onto the silk background fabric. Just attach the two ends of the letter. Now stitch on the velvet leaves, two smaller ones at the top of the letter - noticing how they overlap the letter. They are attached by a couching thread along the central vein and the veins going across the leaf from the points to where the stem joins the leaf. A double perle thread is couched for the stems.

Pin the extra heavy interfacing in place. Using a small ivy leaf shape, stitch the background leaves with back stitch in a single strand of the silk thread.

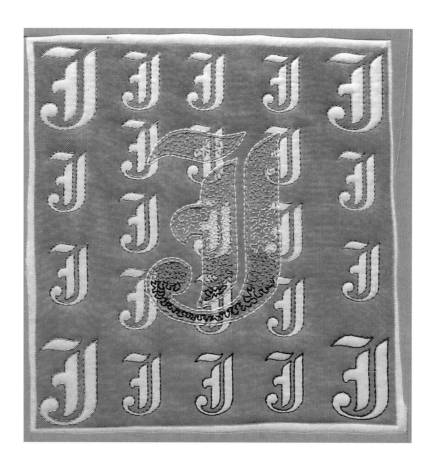

<u>Letter J</u>

This letter J is worked on fabric printed from a design created on a computer.   The background letters are quilted with back stitch using a fine thread.   The large letter J is worked in a medium thickness of thread.

Materials

12" square of cotton fabric
12" square of wadding and backing fabric
1 pack Mulberry silk - fine thickness (any sewing thread could be substituted)
1 pack of similar colour Mulberry silk - medium thickness (any single thread, such as flower thread or coton a broder could be used)

Equipment

Computer, colour printer and design program
12" square wooden embroidery frame
Sharp scissors   Fine embroidery needle

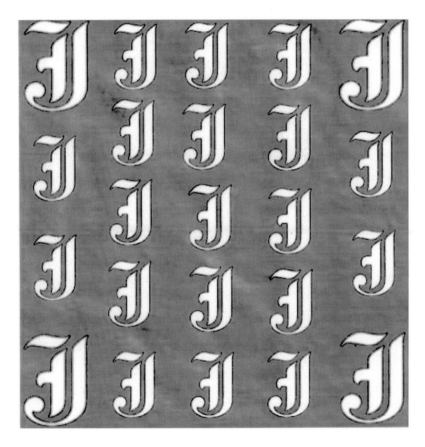

Computer-generated J design, printed onto white cotton fabric

Preparation

Taking an outline of a letter J, the design is prepared by arranging multiple copies of the J in different sizes and, using a paint program on the computer, a coloured background can be created and the resulting design printed onto the cotton fabric.

The wadding is then sandwiched between the printed fabric and the backing and these all tacked together. Stretch onto the frame using either staples or drawing pins. If drawing pins are used, cover the heads with masking tape to avoid the threads catching on them.

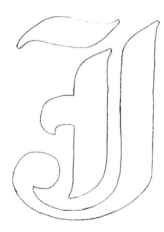

Embroidery

Arrange the fine threads in colour order, starting with the palest. Using this fine thread, backstitch around each of the background letters, starting in one corner with a paler thread and working to the far corner, gradually changing colour.

Change to the medium thickness thread and select five colours to work the large letter.

Again, using the palest shade, outline this letter with back stitch. Work a further line inside the outline in the next shade, also in back stitch. Using a zigzag back stitch, start at the top of the letter and work down a quarter of the way with the second colour. Then gradually introduce the other shades until the whole space is filled.

Letter K

This letter K is worked in pattern darning on evenweave fabric. The darning is worked in three panels with diagonal straight stitch bands in between.

<u>Materials</u>
10" square of evenweave fabric.
DMC Flower thread - 1 skein each of:

Pale Mauve	2209
Deep Mauve	2531
Cerise	2917

(If you have difficulty in getting this thread, any single thread can be substituted.)

<u>Equipment</u>
8" square wooden embroidery frame   Sharp embroidery scissors
No. 24 Tapestry needle

Preparation

Stretch the fabric onto the frame using either staples or drawing pins. If drawing pins are used, it is best to cover the heads with masking tape to avoid the threads catching on them.

Embroidery

Start to work from the central point and outline the letter using the cerise thread, going over and under four threads in running stitch. Work 5 rows on the vertical part of the letter but only 3 rows on the sloping parts.

To get the correct slope, work over 4 threads but, instead of doing a diagonal stitch, count as a true diagonal stitch and move one thread back - see diagram on page 52.

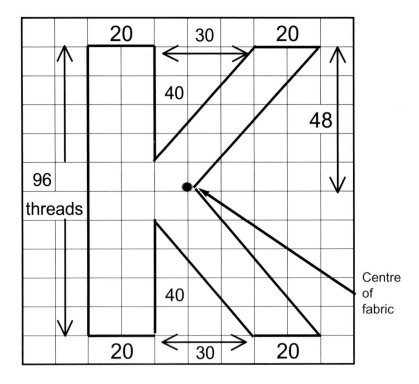

Work the three bands of stitching from the working charts, noting that the first band of diagonal stitches is just 4 threads away from the left-hand side of the letter.

Left side panel

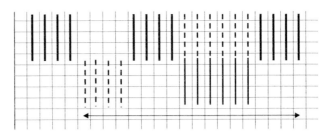

Repeat the section between the arrows twice, i.e. omitting the first four stitches

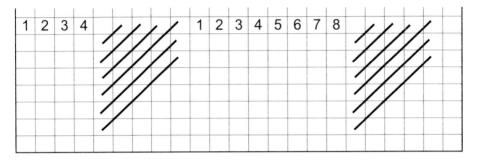

Diagonal stitches between the two side panels and the centre panel

The letter is outlined in rows of running stitches, under and over four threads.

The filling for the centre of the letter is shown in this chart.

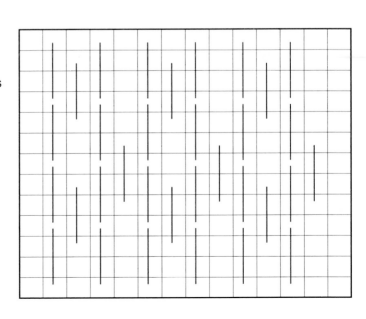

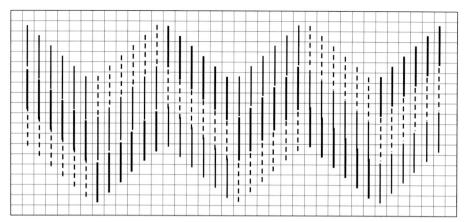

Straight stitches for the right hand side panel.
Repeat these three rows.

Colour Key

Thick: Deep mauve
Thin: Pale mauve
Dotted: Cerise

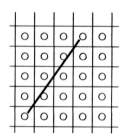

Diagram illustrating
how to achieve the
correct slope for the
arms of the letter K by
stitching horizontally
over four threads and
vertically over five
threads.

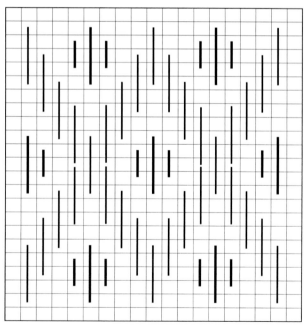

Centre panel stitching

Letter L

The capital letter L is raised and the leaves are wired and stitched using the stumpwork technique. The background is silk and the threads used are called Anchor Marlitt.

Materials
Anchor Marlitt: 1 skein each of

Tan	1003	Orange	1045
Gold	1079	Pale green	1029
Mid green	897		

10" square of silk background fabric

10" square of cotton on which to work the leaves

Piece of felt from which to cut three L shapes

Equipment

8" circular wooden embroidery frame
2 x No. 28 cake wires   Embroidery needle
Tapestry needle   Sharp embroidery scissors
Sharp pencil   Tracing paper

Preparation

Stretch the cotton fabric into the circular frame.   Trace the leaf shapes from
the templates given and place the tracing beneath the fabric and mark the
leaves with a sharp pencil, leaving sufficient space around to cut each leaf
out.   Trace the letter L.

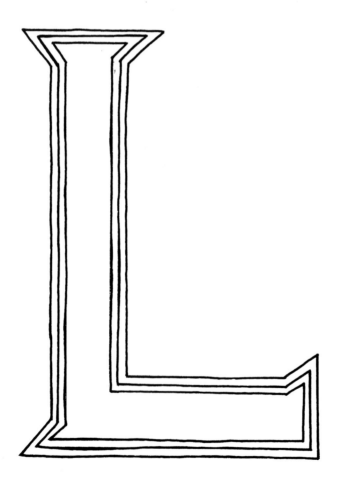

Embroidery

A geranium leaf does not have a central vein so the wiring for these stumpwork leaves just goes round the outside of the leaf.

Couch the wire onto the top of the fabric round the pencil line shapes. Leave about 1" of wire spare at the beginning and end of the shape - these will be used to push through the background fabric and be stitched over to hold the leaves in place on the final embroidery. Blanket stitch over the couched wire, using tiny, neat stitches. - see the diagrams overleaf.

Using long and short stitch, work a row of stitches in pale green, each stitch coming up inside the shape and going down over the wire and inside the loop made by the blanket stitch. Continue to work the remainder of the shape, using long and short stitch, shading the colours and referring to the finished example for the positioning of the colours and the direction of the stitches.

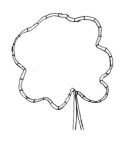  

Wire outline
couched into place
Blanket stitching over the
couched wire
First round of long-and-
short stitch completed

Cut out the leaves, taking great care to cut close to the blanket stitch edge but avoiding cutting the stitches.   Put the three leaves to one side.

Stretch the silk fabric tightly in the circular frame.

Using the traced template, cut out the letter L in felt.

Cut out a second felt shape slightly smaller than the first using the line just inside the outline of the letter L.   Then cut a third shape using the inside line.

Stitch the smallest felt shape in place on the background silk, coming up through the fabric and going down into the felt.   Then stitch the second shape over the top and finally the complete letter shape.

Now work over the padded shape with needlelace.   This consists of rows of blanket stitch - each stitch is "hung" from the loop of the stitch in the previous row and does not go into the felt underneath - see the diagram on page 108 of the Stitch Glossary.

Start each row by bringing the thread up at the edge of the letter, blanket stitching along and then taking the thread back down through the fabric, run it along the back and then up again to commence the next row, always working in the same direction

Carefully push the exposed ends of wire through the silk to position the leaves on the embroidered L.   Stitch the ends firmly in place on the back of the fabric.

Mould the leaves as required to give the chosen effect.

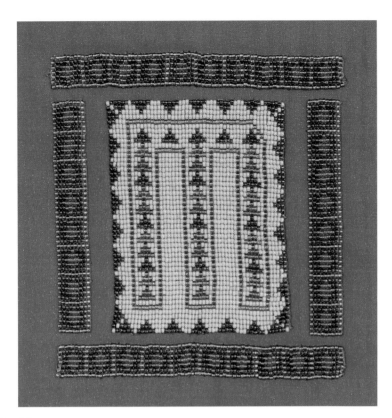

Letter M

This letter is worked using a beading loom and then the beaded sections are attached to a fabric background.

Materials

Seed beads in bronze, gold, turquoise and white
Nymo D Gold beading thread
12" square of turquoise chiffon
12" square of turquoise fabric
12" square of extra heavy interfacing

Equipment

Large beading loom   Beading needle
Sharp embroidery scissors

Preparation

Thread up the beading loom, following the manufacturer's instructions, with 52 threads for the main section.

Sandwich the fabric between the interfacing and the chiffon and tack.

Beading

Following the chart for the main letter section, thread on the beads in rows until the whole section is worked.

Remove from the loom and use the threads to stitch the beading to the centre of the fabric.   Also attach down both sides.

Using the loom again, this time thread up with two lots of 10 threads for the two side sections.   Bead, remove and attach in place at the sides of the letter section as previously.

Finally, thread up the loom again with 82 threads and work the top and lower sections as before.   This time work one and leave a space before you work the second one.   Attach as before.

Two Side Panels

X	X	X	X	X	X	X	X	X	
X	B	B	B	T	B	B	B	X	
X	B	B	T	T	T	B	B	X	
X	B	T	T	T	T	T	B	X	
X	B	B	T	T	T	B	B	X	
X	B	B	B	T	B	B	B	X	
X	X	X	X	X	X	X	X	X	
X	B	B	B	T	B	B	B	X	)
X	B	B	T	T	T	B	B	X	) Repeat these
X	B	T	T	T	T	T	B	X	) six rows
X	B	B	T	T	T	B	B	X	) six times more
X	B	B	B	T	B	B	B	X	)
X	X	X	X	X	X	X	X	X	)

Top and lower panels

Repeat these eight rows nine times more

X	X	X	X	X	X	X	X	X	X	X	X	X	X	X	X	X	X
X	B	B	B	T	B	B	B	X	B	B	B	T	B	B	B	X	
X	B	B	T	T	T	B	B	X	B	B	T	T	T	B	B	X	
X	B	T	T	T	T	T	B	X	B	T	T	T	T	T	B	X	
X	B	B	T	T	T	B	B	X	B	B	T	T	T	B	B	X	
X	B	B	B	T	B	B	B	X	B	B	B	T	B	B	B	X	
X	X	X	X	X	X	X	X	X	X	X	X	X	X	X	X	X	X

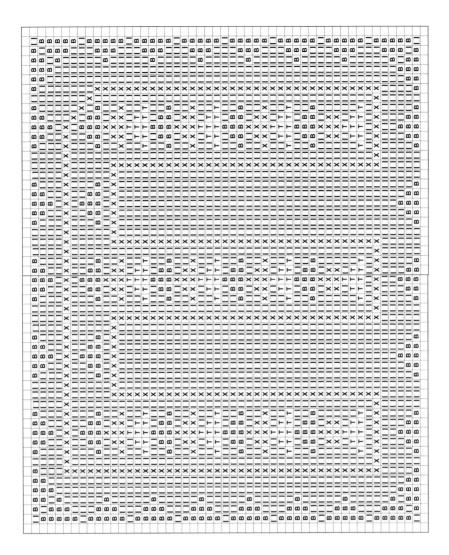

Key to bead colours

B		Bronze			
X		Gold			
T		Turquoise			
I I		White			

Letter N

This letter is worked in a technique called 'pulled thread work' where the stitching thread pulls the fabric threads together. This technique is often confused with drawn thread work, in which threads are actually withdrawn from the fabric.

Traditionally, pulled thread embroidery is stitched with threads of the same colour as the fabric.

60

Materials

11" square of white evenweave fabric
Anchor cotton Perle No. 8 in white
11" square of red cotton fabric to be used as a background
Extra heavy interfacing 7" x 6½ "

Equipment

9" circular wooden embroidery frame
Sharp embroidery scissors
No. 24 tapestry needle   Sewing needle

Preparation

Stretch the evenweave fabric in the frame and mark the central point.

Embroidery

The letter is voided by surrounding it with four-sided stitch - see the following page for instructions on working this stitch.

Follow the chart for the position of the stitches - each one is worked over four threads.

Work star stitches - five each side - between the corner extensions.

The whole design is surrounded by a border of straight stitches, each over four threads, two threads apart.

The final border is a double row of four-sided stitch.

Cut the evenweave fabric about 5/8" away from the outside row of stitching and turn the edge under close to the last row.

Stretch the background fabric into the frame and tack the extra heavy interfacing centrally underneath it.

Stitch the embroidery to the red fabric, catching the outer edges of the four-sided stitches.

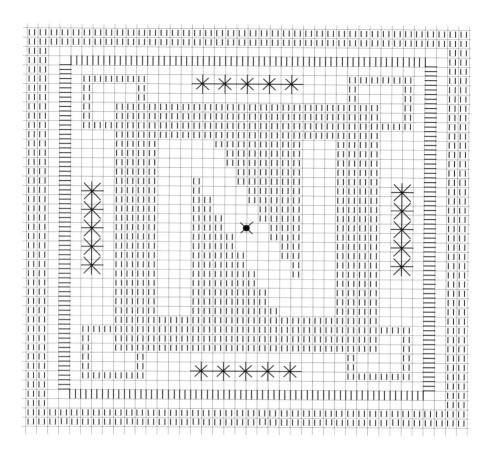

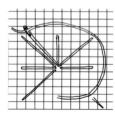

As shown in the chart above, there are five of these Star Stitches on each side of the letter N.

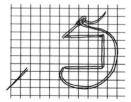

Surrounding the letter N, the area is filled with Four-sided Stitch.

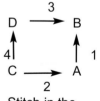

Stitch in the order:
A to B
C to A
D to B and
C to D

62

Letter O

The letter O is worked using massed French knots for the fruit and long-and-short stitch shading for the leaves.   Bondaweb has been used for the applied letter and two fabric corners of the design.   The other two corners have been quilted with back stitch.   The fruit in the centre has been Trapunto padded.   There are many fabrics with fruit designs, so there is no problem if the fabric in the stitched example is not available.

Materials

> 12" square of cotton background fabric
> 8" square of Vilene extra heavy interfacing
> DMC Coton Perle No. 8 - 1 ball each of:
> > Orange   740, 741 & 742
> > Tan   435

Pearsalls Filoselle Embroidery Silk - 1 skein each of:
      Sage Green   189, 191 & 193
1 reel Gutermann Sewing Thread
      Orange 285
Small piece of patterned fabric with oranges
Small square of deeper orange cotton fabric for the letter O
Small square of green patterned fabric for backing the letter
Bondaweb

Equipment

9" circular wooden embroidery frame   Tracing paper
Fine embroidery needle   Sharp pencil
Sharp embroidery scissors

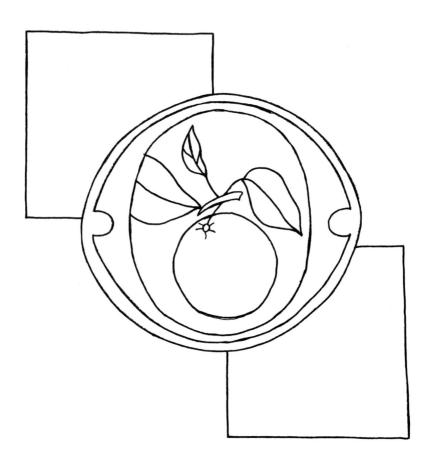

Preparation

Stretch the background fabric tightly onto the frame.

Trace the orange shape and surrounding leaves and position the tracing under the centre of the fabric and draw the design onto the fabric.

Embroidery

Embroider the orange in French knots, starting around the outside with the deepest orange and working to the centre with the mid-orange and then the yellow orange, leaving a small space for the tan marking, where the stem holds the fruit.

Outline the leaves with two strands of the darkest green and then start the shading in this colour, using only a single strand, gradually getting to the lightest green in the centre of the leaves.   Work the veins in the darkest green, using chain stitch.   The branch is worked in rows of stem stitch in the palest green.

Trace the two letter shapes onto the back of the Bondaweb.   Select and cut out two squares of the patterned fabric.   Bondaweb these shapes and trim to size.

Lay the background shape of the letter onto the fabric around the embroidery and position the corner squares and Bondaweb them in place.

Add the letter background and top layer.   The letter is then outlined with the three orange perle threads, couched with the sewing thread.   Zigzag with back stitch to fill the spaces inside the letter.

For the other two quilted corner areas, cut out two or three small leaf shapes in card and use these to mark out the leaves.

Use 5p, 10p and £1 coins to mark out the oranges.   If necessary, mark out with tiny dots.   Quilt along these lines using the Gutermann sewing thread and back stitch.

The work is now ready to be stretched and mounted.

Letter P

The letter P is worked in Pearsalls silk on a cream silk background. Long
and short stitch is used to give a shaded effect to the flower and leaves.

The actual letter is worked in one colour using rows of stem stitch.

Materials

10" square of cream silk
10" square of cotton backing
Pearsalls Filoselle embroidery silk:

1 skein each of:	Rose	085
	Military red	304
	Brick red	305
	Orange yellow	156
	Sage green	190
	Sage green	192
	Sage green	193
2 skeins of:	Navy blue	276

Extra heavy interfacing
Double mount

Equipment

10" square wooden embroidery frame   Sharp embroidery scissors
Fine embroidery needle

Preparation

Tack the silk fabric and cotton backing together and attach to the frame using silk pins.   Trace the design, place over the silk and tack along the design lines.   The paper can then be removed leaving the tacked design.

Embroidery

Outline the petals of the flower in back stitch using two strands of the deepest red silk.   This will give the finished embroidery a raised edge.

Starting with a single strand of the same colour silk, work the first row of long and short stitches around each petal, remembering to note where the petal is folded over.   Work with the other three colours gradually getting paler and making sure that each colour merges well with the previous one.

The flower centre is worked with navy blue bullion knots and has pale green straight stitches between them.   The stamens are just straight stitches in the navy blue silk.

The stem and leaves are then outlined, again with two strands, using the palest green silk.   The central vein is also worked in back stitch.

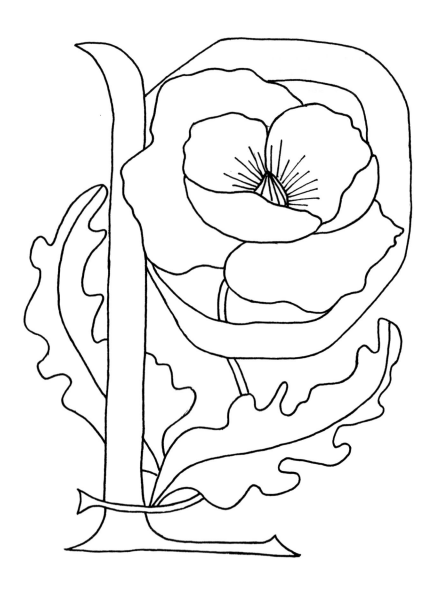

Remember to keep the shading stitches at a sharp angle to the vein and work in a single thread from light on the outside to dark by the vein. The flower stem is worked in stem stitch.

The whole of the letter is worked in rows of navy blue stem stitch.

Letter Q

This letter uses our ribbon embroidery technique for the decoration. For the letter itself, beads and French knots lie within the edging of chain stitch.

Materials

A selection of 3 mm ribbons, including embroidery ribbon and double satin.
Oddments of threads - stranded cotton, silk, coton a broder, etc.
No. 11 seed beads
10" square of cotton fabric

Equipment

8" circular wooden embroidery frame	Fine embroidery needle
Sharp embroidery scissors	Beading needle
Sharp pencil	No. 24 tapestry needle

Preparation

Stretch the fabric tightly in the frame.   Place the design under the fabric and, with a sharp pencil, mark out the position of the gathered ribbon and the ribbon roses.

Embroidery

Start by working the gathered ribbon petals where the dots on the design indicate.   Lengths of 1¼" ribbon are gathered - see instructions in the Stitch Glossary for how to do this.   For the large flowers, each gathered ribbon forms a petal and, on the tall stems, each one forms a small flower.

The foundation for the woven roses is worked using a single thread - coton a broder is a suitable thickness.   Make seven straight stitches, each about ¼" long at a central point to form the spokes of a wheel.   The ribbon is then woven under and over these threads as indicated in the diagrams in the Stitch Glossary - see page 109.

French knot centres are added to the large flowers and also between the ribbons on the tall flowers;   these also have small straight green stitches at a sharp angle to the stem.   Small flowers are then added using French knots and bullion knots.   Small straight stitches are placed around the design to give the impression of foliage and stems are added using stem stitch.

The letter is outlined with three rows of chain stitch.   The area inside is filled with beads, French knots and small flower shapes, which are produced by stitching on a seed bead and coming up about 1/8" outside and stitching into the bead all round.

A quilted background is added inside the letter, stitching to make small triangles.

For more details of this type of ribbon work see
"Ribbon Embroidery" by Daphne J. Ashby & Jackie Woolsey, published by David & Charles, Newton Abbot, Devon - September 1996

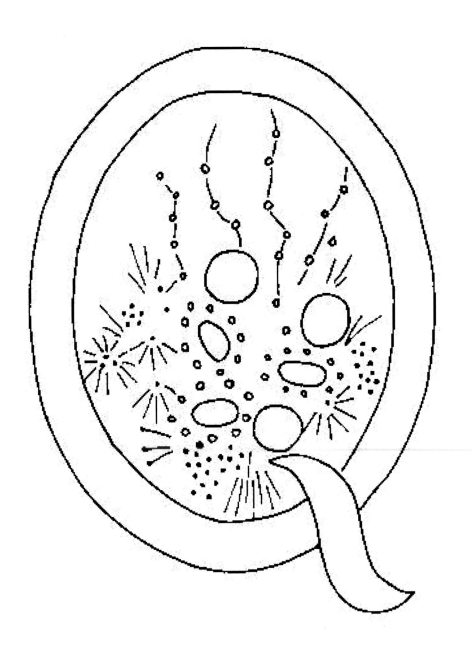

71

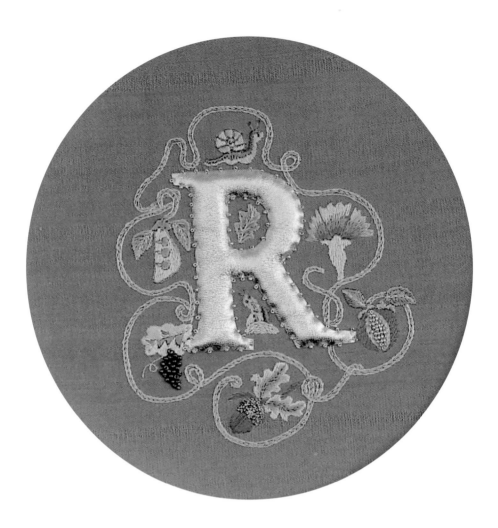

Letter R

This letter is worked in an Elizabethan style using typical motifs. This type of work was often found on coifs and bodices, each motif being surrounded by freely scrolling lines.

Materials

> 10" square of coloured silk
> 10" square of cotton backing fabric

Pearsalls Filoselle embroidery silk - one skein each of:

Willow Green	253	Rose	080
" "	255	"	081
" "	256	"	082
Drab	046	Fawn	067
"	048	Chocolate	214

Gutermann sewing thread - gold 968
Petite gold metallic seed beads
Purple seed beads
Sufficient gold kid for the letter
Yellow felt - similar size

Equipment

8" circular wooden embroidery frame   Tracing paper
Fine embroidery needle   Sharp pencil
Sharp embroidery scissors

Preparation

Back the silk with the cotton fabric and tack both together. Stretch them into the circular frame. Trace the letter R and cut it out in the gold kid. Also cut the letter out in felt but make it slightly smaller all round. Trace the surrounding design and the letter and tack the tracing onto the right side of the silk. Tear away the tracing paper.

Embroidery

Stitch the felt into position and lay the kid over the felt. With gold sewing thread, stitch the gold kid down, coming up through the background fabric alongside the letter and going down through the kid, spacing the stitches evenly.

Work the scrolling with chain stitch in Willow Green 255 and then add a row of stem stitch each side in Willow Green 253.

Leaf in the centre of the letter

This leaf is worked in long and short stitch, starting at the outside edge with Willow Green 255 and then working inside with Willow Green 256. The vein is worked in stem stitch using Willow Green 253.

74

Peapod and leaves
The inside of the pod uses long and short stitch in Willow Green 253 and then the three peas are worked in satin-stitch in Willow Green 255. Split stitch round the edge of the pod in Willow Green 256. This thread is also used for the top of the pod. Start working the leaves from the outside with 255 and complete with 256. The central and side veins are worked in 253.

Carnation
The calyx is worked in long and short stitch in 253. The petals are worked from the top using Rose 080, followed by Rose 081 and finished with 082.

Oak leaves and acorn
Starting from the outside, the leaves are back stitched in 253 and this colour starts the shading. The leaf shading is finished in 255 and the central vein is worked in chain stitch with 256. The acorn is satin-stitched in Chocolate 214 and the cup is worked in French knots using two strands each of Drab 046 and 048. The stem is worked in stem stitch using 214.

Pomegranate
The area surrounding the beads has two rows of chain stitch in Fawn 067 and the rest of the fruit uses the same stitch but is worked in Rose 082. The petite gold seed beads fill the resulting space. The calyx is worked in satin-stitch using 255. The leaves are outlined and stitched in 256 and finished with 255, using long and short stitch. A chain stitch vein is worked in 253.

Grapes and leaves
The outside of the leaves are worked in 253 in satin-stitch and the inside vein shapes in 255. The central vein is chain stitched in 253. The tendril is worked in the same thread in whipped back stitch. Seed beads are then added for the grapes.

The worm-like creature
This is long and short stitched in Drab 046 and the markings, eyes and feelers in Drab 048. The post is satin-stitched in 048 and the mound uses Willow Green 253 and chain stitch.

Snail
The body and head are worked in satin-stitch - the darker Drab 048 at the top and the lighter Drab 046 underneath. The shell is worked in satin-stitch sections in Fawn 067 and then top stitched in Drab 048.

A petite gold bead is then added on top of each of the stitches surrounding the letter.

Letter S

The letter S designed for this example is a very fancy shape, so a simple chain stitch has been used throughout.   The chain stitch is worked with a single strand of Art Silk thread.   The Rajmahal Art Silk (Viscose-stranded) is obtainable from The Needlecraft Centre at Longleat - see the Suppliers' Addresses on page 112.

<u>Materials</u>

10" square of red cotton fabric

1 skein each of Rajmahal Art Silk in:

Gold	45
Bright yellow	144
Pale yellow	91
Green	421
Green	521 (slightly brighter)

Madeira No. 6 - gold 43   )
DMC No. 8 perle thread 3348) for couched edging

<u>Equipment</u>

8" circular wooden embroidery frame
Sharp embroidery scissors
Fine embroidery needle
Tracing paper
Sharp pencil

<u>Preparation</u>

Trace the design.   Stretch the fabric tightly into the frame.   Place the tracing paper on top and tack round the design with small stitches.   Run the needle along the traced lines and peel away the paper.   The tacking stitches can be removed as it is stitched over.

<u>Embroidery</u>

Starting on the outside edge of the "S", work with the gold 45 thread in a single strand and using chain stitch.

Several rows of each colour will be needed to fill the wider parts of the letter. The three yellows will be used to complete the letter.   The two greens are used for the scrolling design.

Outline the letter with the Madeira No. 6 gold 43 thread couched in place and the green scrolling is couched with the DMC No. 8 perle thread 3348, using the nearest of the silk threads to couch.

Letter T

The letter T uses the technique known as "Colour Through Gold". Worked on Congress cloth, Indian rayon threads in rainbow colours are overlaid with gold metallic threads.

Materials

       6" x 8½" piece of Congress cloth
       Indian rayon threads in red, orange, yellow, green, pale blue,
           navy blue & mauve
       1 reel Madeira Gold metallic thread No. 12, colour 33

Key to colours used in chart:

Border of two-colour Cushion Stitches over eight threads

Y	Yellow
YG	Yellow & Green
GB	Green & Pale Blue
O	Orange
OY	Orange & Yellow
RO	Red & Orange
B	Pale Blue
BN	Pale Blue & Navy Blue
N	Navy Blue
G	Green
NM	Navy Blue & Mauve
M	Mauve
MR	Mauve & Red
R	Red

Rice Stitches over four threads, corners crossed with metallic gold:

1	Red
2	Red & Orange
3	Orange
4	Orange & Yellow
5	Yellow
6	Yellow & Green
7	Green
8	Green & Pale Blue
9	Pale Blue
10	Pale Blue & Navy Blue
11	Navy Blue
12	Navy Blue & Mauve
13	Mauve

Cross-stitch chart:

Left	1	2	3	4	5	6	7	8	9	10	11	12	13	14	15	16	Right
Top labels	OY	OY		O		RO		R		MR		MR		M			Gold
Y	1	1	1	2	2	2	3	3	3	4	4	4	5	5	5	6	NM
Y	1	1	2	2	2	3	3	3	4	4	4	5	5	5	6	6	NM
YG	1	2	2	2	3	3	3	4	4	4	5	5	5	6	6	6	NM
YG	2	2													6	7	NM
YG	2	2	Red	Red	Red	Red	Red	Red	Red	Red	Red	Red			7	7	N
YG	2	3	Red	Red	Red	Red	Red	Red	Red	Red	Red	Red			7	7	N
G	3	3	Red	Red	Red	Red	Red	Red	Red	Red					7	8	BN
G	3	3	4	4	4	5	Red	Red	Red	Red	6	7	7	7	8	8	BN
GB	3	4	4	4	5	5	Red	Red	Red	Red	7	7	7	8	8	8	BN
GB	4	4	4	5	5	5	Red	Red	Red	Red	7	7	8	8	8	9	BN
GB	4	4	5	5	5	6	Red	Red	Red	Red	7	8	8	8	9	9	B
GB	4	5	5	5	6	6	Red	Red	Red	Red	8	8	8	9	9	9	B
B	5	5	5	6	6	6	Red	Red	Red	Red	8	8	9	9	9	10	GB
B	5	5	6	6	6	7	Red	Red	Red	Red	8	9	9	9	10	10	GB
BN	5	6	6	6	7	7	Red	Red	Red	Red	9	9	9	10	10	10	GB
BN	6	6	6	7	7	7	Red	Red	Red	Red	9	9	10	10	10	11	GB
BN	6	6	7	7	7	8	Red	Red	Red	Red	9	10	10	10	11	11	G
BN	6	7	7	7	8	8	Red	Red	Red	Red	10	10	10	11	11	11	G
N	7	7	7	8	8	8	Red	Red	Red	Red	10	10	11	11	11	12	YG
N	7	7	8	8	8	9	Red	Red	Red	Red	10	11	11	11	12	12	YG
NM	7	8	8	8	9	9					11	11	11	12	12	12	YG
NM	8	8	8	9	9	9	10	10	10	11	11	11	12	12	12	13	YG
NM	8	8	9	9	9	10	10	10	11	11	11	12	12	12	13	13	Y
NM	8	9	9	9	10	10	10	11	11	11	12	12	12	13	13	13	Y
Bottom labels	M		MR		MR		R		RO		O		OY		OY		Gold

Left-top and right-top corners: **Gold**; Left-bottom and right-bottom corners: **Gold**

Navy Blue Rhodes Stitch over four threads

Pale Blue Rhodes Stitch over four threads

Gold — Gold metallic Rhodes Stitch over eight threads

Red — Red Rhodes Stitch over eight threads

81

Equipment

6" x 8½" rectangular wooden embroidery frame
Sharp embroidery scissors
No. 24 tapestry needle

Preparation

Stretch the Congress cloth tightly onto the frame and attach using either
staples or drawing pins; if pins are used, it is best to cover the heads with
masking tape to avoid the threads catching on them.

Embroidery

Throughout this design, the coloured threads will be used in six thicknesses
(three thicknesses in the needle doubled to give six) and the gold metallic
thread doubled to give two thicknesses.

Mark the vertical centre of the Congress cloth and, measuring the half-way
point, work four Rhodes stitches in red over eight threads above the central
point and four below for the upright part of the T. Then add two more of the
same stitches each side of the top Rhodes stitch.

The entire letter is then surrounded by Rhodes stitch over four threads in
navy blue.

Following the chart, work the rice stitches around the letter, working all the
initial crosses in the coloured threads as indicated and all the corner stitches
in the gold metallic thread.

Next the navy border can be worked, which will then give the positions for
the remaining stitching.

The two-colour cushion stitches used in the border are over eight threads
and do not have any overlaying stitches. All the coloured triangles will have
four stitches, which will leave three stitches for the gold thread.

Four gold Rhodes stitches over eight threads are worked in the corners.

All that remains now is to add the pale blue Rhodes stitches over four
threads that complete the borders.

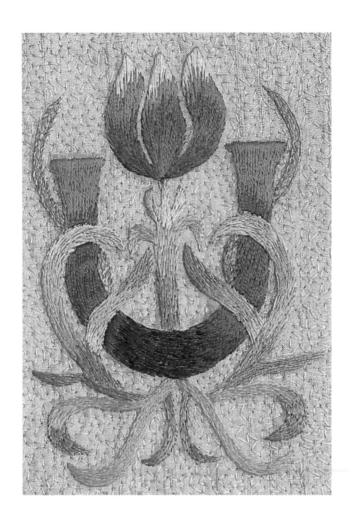

Letter U

For this letter, a William-Morris style design is used and worked in surface stitchery using Pearsalls Filoselle embroidery silk.

Materials

       10" square of cream silk
       10" square of cotton backing fabric
       7" x 3" piece of Vilene extra heavy interfacing
       1 reel Gutermann silk - cream

Pearsalls Filoselle Embroidery Silk -
1 skein each of:

Rose	080	Apple green	009
Rose	082A	Apple green	011
Rose	085	Apple green	013
Indian Pink	038		

Equipment

8" circular wooden embroidery frame   Sharp pencil
Fine embroidery needle   Tracing paper
Sharp embroidery scissors

Preparation

Tack the backing fabric onto the cream silk and stretch them into the circular frame. Trace the design and place the tracing on the top of the silk and back stitch with the cream thread around the design. Tear away the tracing paper.

Embroidery

The areas 1-10 and the letter U are worked in long and short stitch shading. Areas 1, 2 and 3 start with Rose 080, then 082A is used and finally 085. The letter U starts at the top with 082A, then 085 and finally Indian Pink 038 at the base of the letter. In areas 4 and 5, start with the palest Apple green 009 at the top and work down using 011 and 013.

Areas 6 and 7 use the same colours but start at the top with the deepest green 013. For 8 & 9, start with the deepest green at the outside edges and start 10 with the palest green at the top, just below the flower. See the photograph for the placing of the colours.

Areas A and B have a row of chain stitch in green 011 and are outlined with a row of stem stitch in 013. C, D, E and F are worked in rows of stem stitch in 013. G and H are also in stem stitch but using mid-green 011.

The letter is now complete but the example in the photograph was finished off by placing the piece of extra heavy interfacing behind the embroidery and, using the cream silk thread, the background area was zig-zag stitched around the embroidery using back stitch.

84

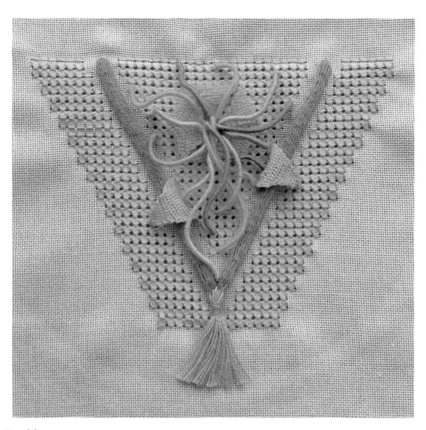

Letter V

This letter is worked in Casalguidi style. Casalguidi embroidery was originally worked in the late 19th century in the village by that name near Pistoia in Italy and was worked on linen.

Material

10" square of evenweave fabric in cream
DMC Coton Perle No. 8:

1 ball each in:		
	Fawn	738
	Tan	435
	Orange	741
	Variegated Green	94

10" square deep orange fabric for the backing
Extra heavy interfacing

Equipment

8" circular wooden embroidery frame   Embroidery needle
Sharp embroidery scissors   No. 24 tapestry needle

Preparation

Stretch the fabric tightly into the frame.

Embroidery

Starting 2" from the left side of the frame and about 3" down, work the four-sided stitch background following the chart and using the fawn perle thread.

The letter V is worked as a padded, raised stem band. Begin by cutting 10 lengths of the tan thread each 14" long, to make the thread padding.

Fold the threads in half and sew the looped end in the centre of the unworked space between the four-sided stitch and level with the top. Couch this in place with stitiches about ¼" apart - see photograph below.

Cover the thread padding with satin-stitch (using the embroidery needle) and the fawn thread as shown in the photograph below.

Work a foundation of stitches over the satin-stitch, each stitch about ¼" apart - see the photograph at the top of page 89.

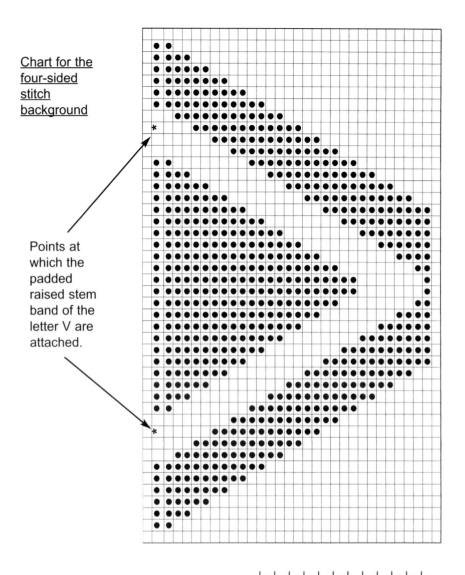

Chart for the four-sided stitch background

Points at which the padded raised stem band of the letter V are attached.

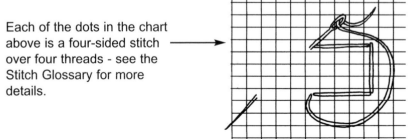

Each of the dots in the chart above is a four-sided stitch over four threads - see the Stitch Glossary for more details.

88

Work stem stitch in tan coton perle taking one stitch over each bar of foundation stitches. Always work in the same direction. Use the tapestry needle for this and push each row over as it is worked to ensure the whole surface is covered - see photograph below. Make sure you do not split the thread of the foundation bars.

Work the second side of the letter in the same way and, when the whole of that band is covered, gather the ends from each band together and stitch over them several times to form a tassel. Cut the ends evenly.

The orange 'flower' shapes are worked in needlelace - see the diagram on page 108 of the Stitch Glossary. Start by stitching two long stitches each about ¾" long on top of each other. Then a row of blanket stitches are worked over the double thread - about 14 in all.

Keep working the rows into the loops of the previous row, decreasing by one stitch on each row to form a triangle. At the point of the triangle, go into the background fabric - fasten off. Work six shapes in this way in the orange perle thread.

Work two more shapes over the V bands - this time in green - starting with two longer stitches and working 18 blanket stitches. See the photograph of the finished letter for the positions.

The work is finished by wrapping threads to decorate the work. Eight threads are used as the core and then wrapped with a single thread. Make several of these using all the colours that have been used in the embroidery.

For further details of Casalguidi work see the publication:
"Casalguidi Style Linen Embroidery" by Effie Mitrofanis
published by Kangaroo Press   ISBN 0 86417 755 0

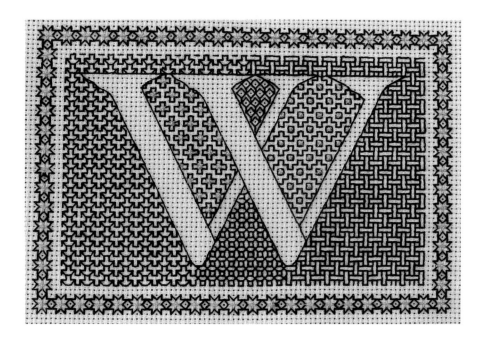

Letter W

The letter W is worked using traditional blackwork stitches. Blackwork, which became popular in Tudor times, is either worked by stitching the subject and leaving the background plain or by stitching the background and voiding the subject. Gold is quite often added to enhance the work.

Materials

10" x 8" piece of Hardanger fabric

1 skein of DMC Flower Thread in black
If you are unable to obtain flower thread,
any other single thread can be substituted

1 reel Madeira gold metallic thread No. 12, colour 33

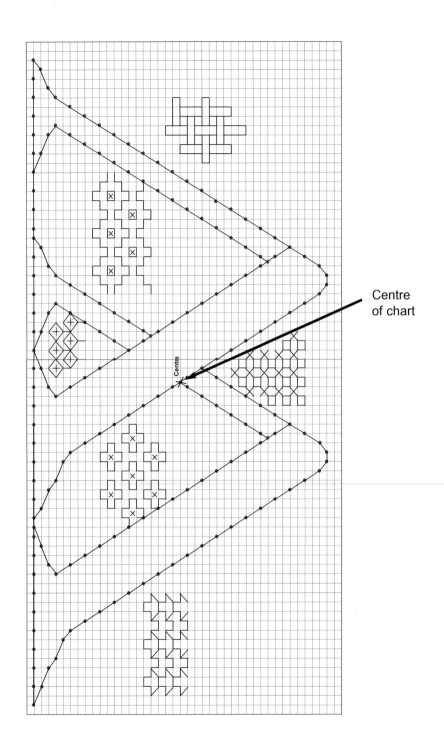

Centre
of chart

Centre

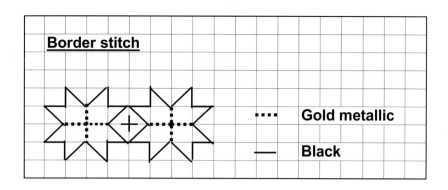

Border stitch

Gold metallic

Black

Equipment

10" x 8" rectangular wooden embroidery frame
Sharp embroidery scissors
No. 12 tapestry needle

Preparation

Stretch the fabric tightly onto the frame and attach using either staples or drawing pins. If drawing pins are used, cover these with masking tape to avoid the threads catching on them.

Embroidery

Starting at the centre, as indicated on the chart, and using a single black thread, outline the letter, noting that some of the stitches go over two squares and others only over one - this is in order to get the slope of the letter at the correct angle.

The shapes that remain are then filled with the blackwork stitches as shown on the chart, again using a single black thread.

Use the gold thread where indicated - just a single thickness.

Throughout the stitched areas, you will find it is necessary sometimes to use half or even part stitches.

Be careful to start the border in the correct place look at the photograph for guidance. Always avoid running the thread behind an unstitched area as it may show through.

Letter X

The letter X is worked entirely in cross stitch and has been adapted from a repeat geometric pattern used as a decoration on the front of a Mexican shirt.

Hardanger fabric is used and the design is stitched in DMC Flower Thread. If you are unable to obtain this thread, any single thread can be substituted.

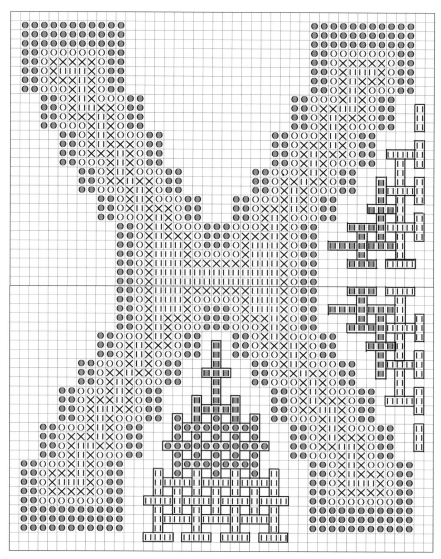

Materials

10" x 8" rectangle of Hardanger fabric

DMC Flower thread in the following colours:

Rust	2919
Fawn green	2673
Deep turquoise	2590
Pale turquoise	2932
Orange	2947

Fine bronze Madeira metallic thread

FOUR CORNER DESIGNS FOR LETTER X
(This is the bottom left-hand corner)

X ~ Start of bottom and side designs

Equipment
10" x 8" rectangular wooden embroidery frame
No. 24 tapestry needle
Sharp embroidery scissors

Preparation
Stretch the fabric tightly onto the rectangular frame and attach using either staples or drawing pins. If drawing pins are used, cover these with masking tape to avoid the threads catching on them.

Embroidery
The embroidery around the letter X is worked in cross stitch but each group of three is outlined in a fine bronze Madeira metallic thread.

Starting with the actual letter X, with a single strand thread in the needle and from the centre of the design, follow the chart, adding the outer panels when the letter has been completed.

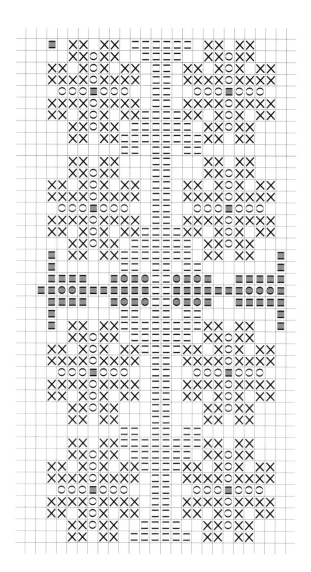

Design chart for the top and bottom panels
of the letter X

Design chart for the
side panels of the
letter X

Key to colours used
in all the charts for
the letter X:

X	Deep Turquoise
▮	Fawn Green
O	Rust
●	Orange
‖	Pale Turquoise

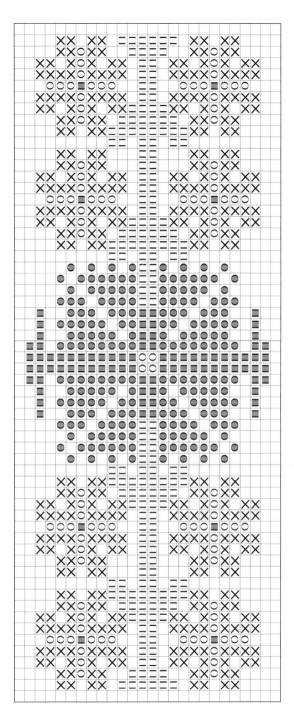

Letter Y

This letter is worked in Hardanger on an evenweave fabric and is stitched in Coton Perle No. 8. The colour of the thread matches the colour of the fabric. The solid stitching of the letter and border is surrounded by an area of withdrawn threads and woven bars.

Materials

12" square of evenweave fabric
12" square of contrasting backing fabric
1 ball of DMC Coton Perle No. 8 in colour to match the evenweave fabric

Equipment

12" square wooden embroidery frame
No. 24 tapestry needle
Sharp pointed embroidery scissors

Preparation

Stretch the fabric on the frame using either staples or drawing pins. If drawing pins are used, it is advisable to cover the heads with masking tape to avoid the threads catching on them.

Embroidery

Start to work at the lower left-hand corner of the letter Y, 5½" in from the left-hand side of the fabric and about 3¼" up from the lower edge.

The chart for working the letter is spread over the following two pages.

Working from the chart on page 101, showing the lower half of the Y, start with four stitches over 12 threads, then four stitches over 8 threads and four stitches over 4 threads. Continue following the chart until the letter is complete.

Next start the area with withdrawn threads in the centre of the letter, withdrawing six threads and leaving four threads alternately. The bars are woven going under two and over two threads.

This technique relies entirely on correct counting of the threads.

To work the outside border, count the threads carefully and stitch the border, remembering there is one extra stitch centrally on both the top and bottom border. This will have to be stitched before the remainder of the central area is worked.

Look up the Hardanger technique in any embroidery book if you have difficulty.

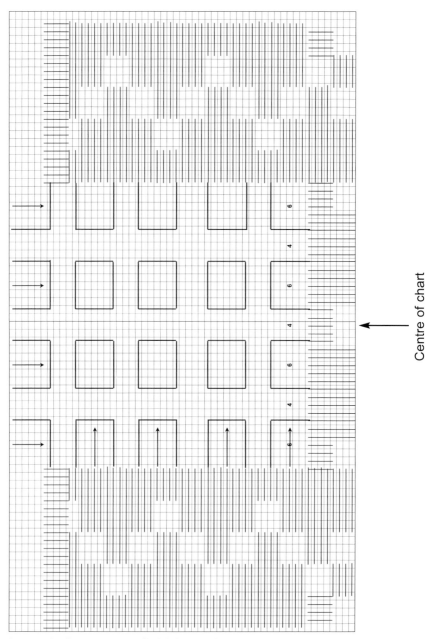

Arrows indicate areas of withdrawn threads:

Six threads are withdrawn both horizontally and vertically, leaving four threads between each group in both directions.

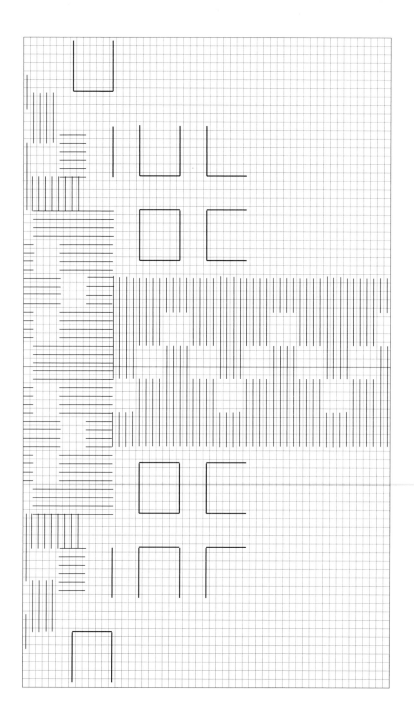

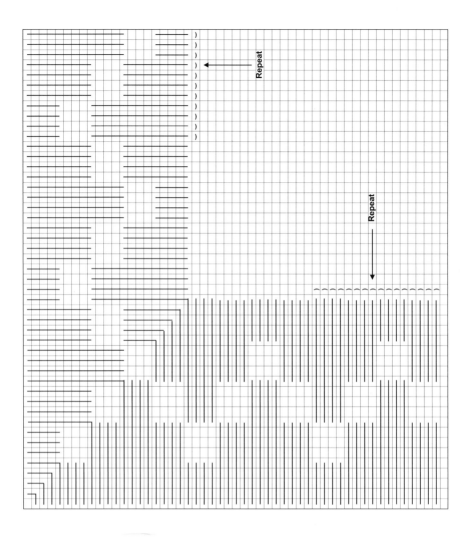

This is the chart for the border surrounding the letter Y:

Repeat the border pattern as shown in the chart but, in the centre of the border, the top and bottom edges will have one extra stitch - this is because the lower section of the "Y" 12/4/4 repeat covers 20 threads, which involves 21 holes.

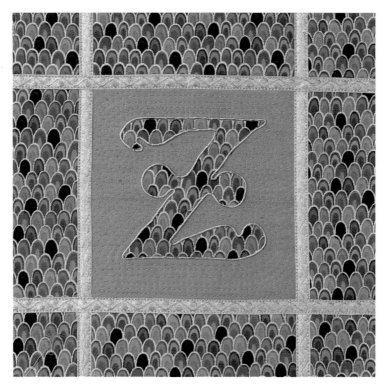

Letter Z

This letter Z, the design of which was taken from a manuscript of the 15th century, has a turquoise silk background and uses a cotton fabric with a colourful but small design.

Materials
        10" square of coloured cotton fabric
        10" square of turquoise silk
        10" square of extra heavy interfacing
        10" square of Bondaweb
        1½ metres of 7 cm gold ribbon
        Japanese gold couching thread
        Gold coloured machine thread

Equipment

        10" rectangular wooden embroidery frame
        Sewing machine
        Fine embroidery needle

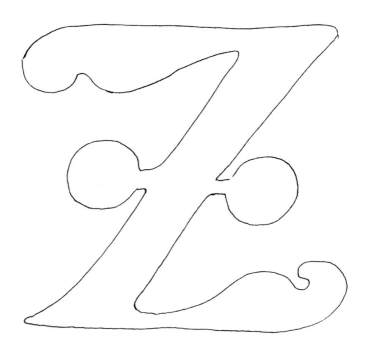

<u>Embroidery</u>

Place a background of extra heavy interfacing behind the silk.

Iron Bondaweb onto the back of the 10" square of cotton fabric and cut out the fancy Z (from the centre of the fabric) and fuse it to the centre of the background silk.   Add a border of the same fabric - see the photograph for the placing of the border fabric.

Machine-stitch a ribbon outline into position to hide the raw edges of the border fabric.

Stretch the background silk onto the embroidery frame - use silk pins to secure this in position.   Hand-quilt the panel behind the letter, the lines of stitching following the shape of the Z.

Finally, couch the Japanese thread around the outline of the letter.

STITCH GLOSSARY

Back Stitch

Blanket Stitch

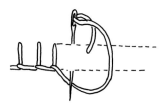

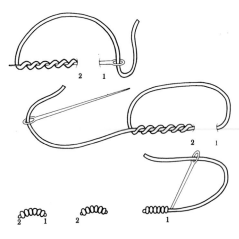

Bullion knot

Chain Stitch

105

Couching

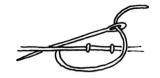

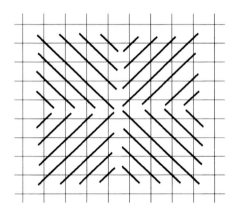

Cushion Stitch
over 8 threads
(canvas work)

Detached Chain Stitch

Fly Stitch

Four-sided Stitch

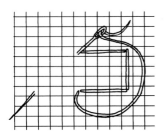

Stitch in the order:
A to B
C to A
D to B and
C to D

French knot

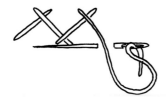

Herringbone Stitch

Long & Short Stitch

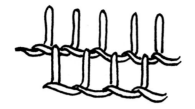

Needle Lace

Rhodes Stitch over four threads

- note that the final stitch, 17 to 18, repeats stitch 1 to 2 but in the opposite direction, i.e on top of stitch 1 to 2.

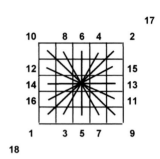

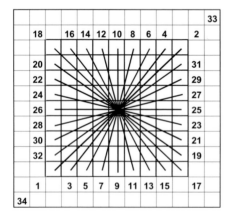

Rhodes Stitch over eight threads

- note that the final stitch, 33 to 34, repeats stitch 1 to 2 but in the opposite direction, i.e on top of stitch 1 to 2.

Rice Stitch

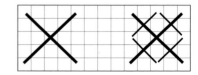

Gathered ribbon petal:

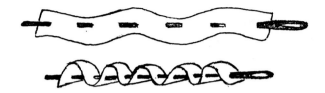

Cut 3mm ribbon into 1¼" lengths. Bring needle containing matching colour cotton up through the fabric and put the needle down in the middle of the ribbon 3mm from one end. Gather the ribbon onto the needle as shown in the diagram.

Put the needle back through its first entry point in the ribbon and back through the fabric, ensuring that the ribbon ends are one on top of the other. As it is pulled through the fabric, the ribbon will gather to make the petal - secure on the reverse with a back stitch.

Woven ribbon rose:

Using a single thread, sew a series of seven straight stitches, each about 6mm long, to form the spokes of a wheel.

Bring a needle threaded with 3mm ribbon up in the centre of the wheel and begin to weave going round under and over the spokes. Pull the ribbon firmly at first and then more loosely towards the outside. Work round as many times as needed to cover the spokes, then take the ribbon through to the back of the work and back stitch through the spokes on the reverse to finish off.

Satin-Stitch

 Seeding Stitch

Split Stitch

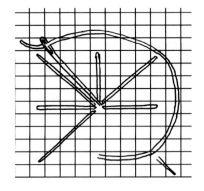 Star Stitch

Stem Stitch

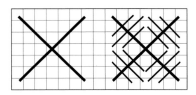 Triple Rice Stitch

Van Dyke Stitch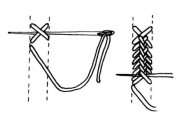

Whipped Back Stitch

Zig-zag Back Stitch

SUPPLIERS' ADDRESSES

A L Maugham & Co. Ltd.   3-9 Fazackerley Street
(off Old Hall Street)
LIVERPOOL L3 9DN
for Gold Kid (letters A, B, G and R)

Mulberry Silks   2 Old Rectory Cottage
Easton Grey
MALMESBURY
Wilts SN16 0PE
01666 840881

The Needlecraft Centre   Stable Courtyard
Longleat
WARMINSTER
BA12 7NL
for Rajmahal Art Silk (Letter S)

Nostalgia   147A Nottingham Road
EASTWOOD
Notts. NG16 3GJ
for Velvet Ivy Leaves (Letter I)

Pearsells Embroidery Silks   Tancred Street
TAUNTON
Somerset TA1 1RY
01823 274700